# RIDE THE LIGHTNING

As recorded by METALLICA on ELEKTRA RECORDS

Management: Q Prime, Inc.
Transcribed by Carl Culpepper
("Fade to Black" transcribed by Kenn Chipkin)
Edited by Jeff Jacobson, Jon Chappell and Mark Phillips
Music Engraving by W.R. Music
Production Manager: Daniel Rosenbaum
Art Direction: Alisa Hill
Administration: Monica Corton
Director of Music: Mark Phillips

*Photography by Ross Halfin/Vereecke*

ISBN: 978-0-89524-494-9

# Ride The Lightning

## INTRODUCTION

Metallica is an extraordinary thrash band. Widely regarded as the "Beatles of speed metal," they are, by far, the most ambitious, inventive and musically satisfying proponents of the genre. In their vision, the possibilities for enlargement and elaboration of the heavy metal medium have been more than glimpsed, they have become practically codified, attaining a contemporary "classic" significance while providing virtually everyone else presently active in the style with a model of how it's done. Emerging in the early 1980's, they rapidly assumed the status of archetype following the release of their second album, *Ride the Lightning*, in 1984.

If Metallica are the "Beatles of speed metal," then *Ride the Lightning* must be perceived as their *"Rubber Soul"* or *"Revolver."* Displaying a richness of compositional/arrangemental technique and a well-honed command of the complexities of the music in all its facets, it is a clearly more evolved (and involved) work, signaling an important transitional point between their early style (as heard on 1983's *Kill 'Em All*) and the shape of things to come (like the monumental *Master of Puppets*, 1986). In *Ride the Lightning*, their manipulation of structural density seems to have developed, exhibited by their approach to guitar orchestration and instrumental texture (they have even seen fit to include a superb instrumental piece, "The Call of Ktulu" in this offering). Guitar harmonies, counterpoint and timbral shadings are more thoughtful and plentiful than ever before. The characteristic eccentricities of the music (unpredictable and radical shifts in tempo, meter, feel, dynamics and tonality) are better integrated into the compositions with the result of making them more accessible. The performances are more spirited and confident: drums, rhythm guitars and bass locking in with a tightness shared only by precision machinery. The recorded sound presents a more polished and produced sonic impression, serving to enhance the numerous details and intricacies of the music without imparting a glossy, over-processed quality. Lyrical imagery and content reveal a stronger tendency towards the socially-conscious subject matter ("Fight Fire with Fire," "Ride the Lightning") with which they are now closely associated as well as an uncanny ability to deal with the unwieldy topics of war, insanity, depression and death ("Fade to Black," "Trapped Under Ice") and even Biblical historical narrative ("Creeping Death"). Though hinted at previously in the repertoires of Black Sabbath, Judas Priest and Iron Maiden, these themes are largely an anomaly in mainstream metal where the bulk of the material is inexorably bound to "sex, drugs and rock 'n' roll." In the songwriting of Metallica, the oddity becomes the norm—and vice versa—with virtually a complete rejection of the patented, well-worn hard rock and metal clichés held dear to the majority of the formula bands of the 1980's.

Harmonically, *Ride The Lightning* is the natural step following *Kill 'Em All*. The unmistakable heavy riffs with typically unusual chord progressions and melodic twists are featured in abundance. Consider the riff found in "Trapped Under Ice" in Coda I. Labeled Rhy. Fig. 5, it contains a number of Metallica ingredients: a mix of power chords, down-picked palm-muted bass notes, odd scale melodies (in this case a Phrygian-Dominant scale—a favorite of Joe Satriani and Yngwie Malmsteen—in bar 2) and the characteristic tritone (flat five) dissonance (emphasized by the chunking rhythmic delivery of a galloping, muted Bb in bar 4). Along similar lines are the chorus riff in "Fight Fire with Fire" (again exploiting an E to Bb tritone dissonance), the verse riff in "Ride the Lightning" (with a Bb5 power chord over a palm-muted low E pedal) and the chorus riff in "For Whom the Bell Tolls" (look for Bb5 again, this time amidst a series of power chords over the recurring triplet motif on open E). An interesting set of variants on the tritone riff is heard in the course of "The Call of Ktulu." Rhy. Fig. 2 is made up of two A minor chords arpeggiated hypnotically with the eerie touch of an A to D# bass line as part of the picking pattern. This in turn yields the distorted versions: Rhy. Fig. 4 in the rhythm guitar combined with the palm-muted arpeggios of Rhy. Fig. 5 (which is a strict restatement of Rhy. Fig. 2 colored with an overdriven sound) and Rhy. Figs. 8 and 10--pure power chord versions of Rhy. Fig. 2. All of which illustrate the effective use of a simple riff idea in terms of both its potential for thematic development and harmonic impact. For further elaborations, guitar improvisation is added over Rhy. Fig. 8, and Rhy. Fig. 10 is mated to Rhy. Fig. 5 (muted, distorted arpeggios) when it reemerges after the guitar solo. Riff manipulation, development and variation are Metallica's strong suits.

Strong also is Metallica's mastery of guitar orchestration. On *Ride the Lightning,* they have refined the technique of overdubbing to a science. Seeming to carry on in this sense from the efforts of the late Randy Rhoads in metal, they have created a distinctive palette of guitar colors through the layering of electric and acoustic timbres on the album. Check out the beautiful acoustic textures in "Fight Fire with Fire" (intro) which generate a mutated Renaissance lute consort mood (made quirky by the changing bars of 3/4 and 2/4) or the moody intro of "Fade to Black" with the tasteful blend of acoustic guitar arpeggiations (Rhy. Figs. 1 and 2) and Kirk Hammett's melodic and introspective electric guitar phrases.

Harmony guitar sections, another aspect of orchestration, grace virtually every track on *Ride the Lightning.* Standout examples can be heard in "Ride the Lightning" (the intro in parallel 4ths and the second half of the guitar solo with its unusual interval changes from 4th to 5ths to mixed 6ths and 4ths in the same line), "For Whom the Bell Tolls" (the interlude, in which the ostinato of Riff A in Gtr. II is joined to the guitar harmony of Gtrs. III and IV to form an unusual trio texture which flirts with melodic independence), "Fade to Black" (the interlude with harmony in parallel 6ths, and Riff A, with harmony in parallel 3rds), "Creeping Death" (the coda with Riff B in parallel 4ths and string bending—reminiscent of the Scorpions) and "The Call of Ktulu" (the coda, which builds through well-planned guitar layering, beginning with Rhy. Fig. 11's power chords, to which are added two guitars in parallel 3rds and then expanded to triad texture in parallel, three-part harmony).

"The Call of Ktulu" sent me digging through my dog-eared copies of H.P. Lovecraft to find the classic horror story from the famous (or infamous) Cthulhu collection. Metallica has done a splendid job of setting this eldritch literary masterpiece to music. H.P. Lovercraft's brooding and oppressive style of storytelling is captured eloquently in the instrumental arrangement, which builds with an appropriately sinister but irresistible series of motifs in the opening sections to the sonic equivalent of a Lovecraftian climax which sneaks up on you like a disembodied tentacle from beyond the cosmos. Try listening to "The Call of Ktulu" after reading the story (spelled "The Call of Cthulhu" and available in various Lovecraft paperback anthologies)—it's an incomparable experience.

Kirk Hammett's guitarwork on *Ride the Lightning* is, as expected, exciting and full of drama. A well-trained player, he is the personification of speed metal energy on the one hand—soloing with a frantic abandon over any conceivable set of convoluted changes at warp-speed tempos—and the model of understatement, taste and restraint on the other hand, coloring the songs with gorgeous overdubbed harmonies or playing hauntingly melodic passages (as in the intro to "Fade to Black," for example) where needed. Regarding the former, he pulls out all stops in the hair-raising guitar solos to "Fight Fire with Fire," "Trapped Under Ice" (three great solo episodes in this one, each acting as forceful instrumental bridges) and "Creeping Death." His style embraces a myriad of modern guitar techniques: two-handed tapping, ostinato riffs, modal/diatonic scale sequencing, sweep and tremolo picking, whammy bar dives and vibrato, blues and hard rock string bending and rhythmic noises. He has a penchant for "building a solo," frequently employing a "compositional" scheme in organizing his improvisations, the end result being one of cohesion and direction with areas of contrast, motivic development and imitation of rhythm figures, melodic contour and textures. He is fond of using the wah wah pedal as a filter/boost (heard on "Fight Fire with Fire," "Trapped Under Ice" and "The Call of Ktulu") as well as varying shades of distortion from full crunch to medium heavy and clean tone. He is the perfect complement to the bone-crunching rhythm section of James Hetfield (guitar), Lars Ulrich (drums) and Cliff Burton (bass). Therein lies the elusive chemistry. Simple to state, impossible to express in words alone, Metallica's music must be experienced to be appreciated—it is immediate, thought-provoking and utterly without mercy.

- Wolf Marshall

# CONTENTS

# TABLATURE EXPLANATION

**TABLATURE:** A six-line staff that graphically represents the guitar fingerboard, with the top line indicating the highest sounding string (high E). By placing a number on the appropriate line, the string and fret of any note can be indicated. The number 0 represents an open string.

| | |
|---|---|
| 1st string - High E | |
| 2nd string - B | |
| 3rd string - G | |
| 4th string - D | |
| 5th string - A | |
| 6th string - Low E | |

5th string, 3rd fret

1st string, 15th fret,
2nd string, 15th fret,
played together

an open E chord

## Definitions for Special Guitar Notation

**BEND:** Strike the note and bend up ½ step (one fret).

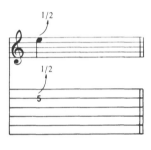

**BEND:** Strike the note and bend up a whole step (two frets).

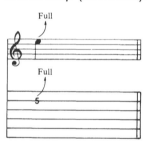

**BEND AND RELEASE:** Strike the note and bend up ½ (or whole) step, then release the bend back to the original note. All three notes are tied, only the first note is struck.

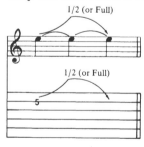

**PRE-BEND:** Bend the note up ½ (or whole) step, then strike it.

**PRE-BEND AND RELEASE:** Bend the note up ½ (or whole) step. Strike it and release the bend back to the original note.

**UNISON BEND:** Strike the two notes simultaneously and bend the lower note up to the pitch of the higher.

**VIBRATO:** The string is vibrated by rapidly bending and releasing the note with the left hand or tremolo bar.

**WIDE OR EXAGGERATED VIBRATO:** The pitch is varied to a greater degree by vibrating with the left hand or tremolo bar.

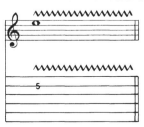

**SLIDE:** Strike the first note and then slide the same left-hand finger up or down to the second note. The second note is not struck.

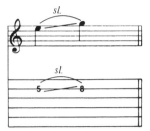

**SLIDE:** Same as above, except the second note is struck.

**SLIDE:** Slide up to the note indicated from a few frets below.

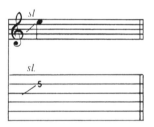

**SLIDE:** Strike the note and slide up or down an indefinite number of frets, releasing finger pressure at the end of the slide.

**PICK SLIDE:** The edge of the pick is rubbed down the length of the string producing a scratchy sound.

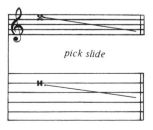

**HAMMER-ON:** Strike the first (lower) note, then sound the higher note with another finger by fretting it without picking.

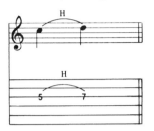

**HAMMER-ON:** Without picking, sound the note indicated by sharply fretting the note with a left-hand finger.

**PULL-OFF:** Place both fingers on the notes to be sounded. Strike the first note and without picking, pull the finger off to sound the second (lower) note.

**TRILL:** Very rapidly alternate between the note indicated and the small note shown in parentheses by hammering on and pulling off.

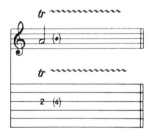

**TAPPING:** Hammer ("tap") the fret indicated with the right-hand index or middle finger and pull off to the note fretted by the left hand.

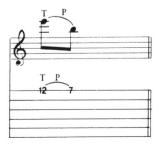

**TREMOLO PICKING:** The note is picked as rapidly and continuously as possible.

**RAKE:** Drag the pick across the strings indicated from low to high with a single downward motion.

**ARPEGGIO:** Play the notes of the chord indicated by quickly rolling them from bottom to top.

**NATURAL HARMONIC:** Strike the note while the left hand lightly touches the string over the fret indicated.

**ARTIFICIAL HARMONIC:** The note is fretted normally and a harmonic is produced by adding the edge of the thumb or the tip of the index finger of the right hand to the normal pick attack. High volume or distortion will allow for a greater variety of harmonics.

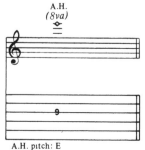

**TREMOLO BAR:** The pitch of the note or chord is dropped a specified number of steps then returned to the original pitch.

**PALM MUTING:** The note is partially muted by the right hand lightly touching the string(s) just before the bridge.

**MUFFLED STRINGS:** A percussive sound is produced by laying the left hand across the strings without depressing them and striking them with the right hand.

**RHYTHM SLASHES:** Strum chords in rhythm indicated. Use chord voicings found in the fingering diagrams at the top of the first page of the transcription.

**RHYTHM SLASHES (SINGLE NOTES):** Single notes can be indicated in rhythm slashes. The circled number above the note name indicates which string to play. When successive notes are played on the same string, only the fret numbers are given.

# Definitions of Musical Symbols

| | |
|---|---|
| *8va* | Play an octave higher than written |
| *15ma* | Play two octaves higher than written |
| *loco* | Play as written |
| *pp (pianissimo)* | Very soft |
| *p (piano)* | Soft |
| *mp (mezzo - piano)* | Moderately soft |
| *mf (mezzo - forte)* | Moderately loud |
| *f (forte)* | Loud |
| *ff (fortissimo)* | Very loud |
| (accent) | Accentuate note (play it louder) |
| (accent) | Accentuate note with great intensity |
| (staccato) | Play note short |
| / | Repeat previous beat (used for quarter or eighth notes) |
| // | Repeat previous beat (used for sixteenth notes) |
| ∕. | Repeat previous measure |
| ‖: :‖ | Repeat measures between repeat signs |
| ‖: \|1. :‖ \|2. | When a repeated section has different endings, play the first ending only the first time and the second ending only the second time. |
| *D.S. al Coda* | Go back to the sign (𝄋), then play until the measure marked "To Coda," then skip to the section labeled "Coda." |
| *D.C. al Fine* | Go back to the beginning of the song and play until the measure marked "Fine" (end). |

**NOTE:** Tablature numbers in parentheses mean:

1. The note is being sustained over a barline (note in standard notation is tied), or

2. The note is sustained, but a new articulation (such as a hammer-on, pull-off, slide or vibrato) begins, or

3. The note is a barely audible "ghost" note (note in standard notation is also in parentheses).

# FIGHT FIRE WITH FIRE

Words and Music by
James Hetfield, Lars Ulrich, and
Cliff Burton

*Two gtrs. arr. for one.

*Vol. swell with increasing distortion

*Downstemmed guitar is notated to the right of slashes.

*Additional Lyrics*

2. Blow the universe into nothingness.
   Nuclear warfare shall lay us to rest. *(To Chorus)*

3. Time is like a fuse, short and burning fast.
   Armageddon is here, like said in the past. *(To Chorus)*

4. Soon to fill our lungs, the hot winds of death.
   The gods are laughing, so take your last breath. *(To Chorus)*

# RIDE THE LIGHTNING

Words and Music by
James Hetfield, Lars Ulrich,
Cliff Burton and Dave Mustaine

17

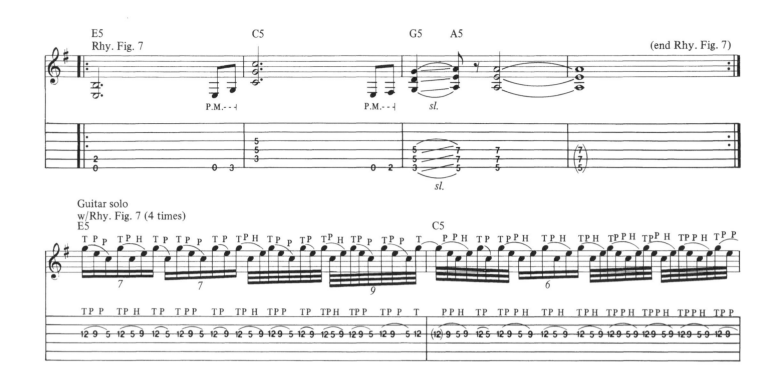

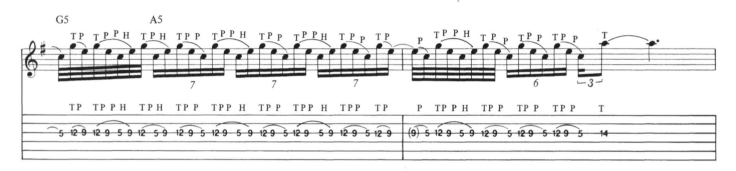

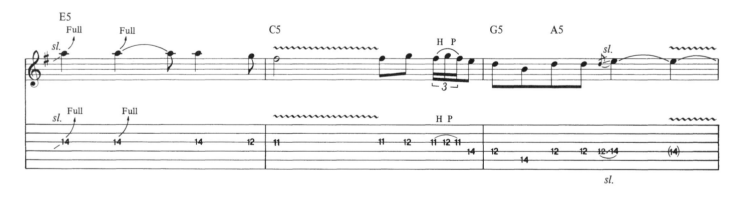

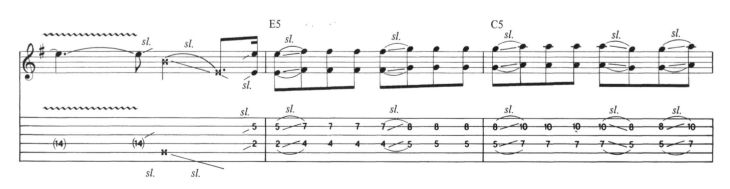

*Bend refers to both gtrs.

w/Rhy. Fig. 6 (1st 3 bars only)

*Lower gtr. indicated to right of slashes in TAB.

w/Rhy. Fig. 6 (1st 3 bars only)

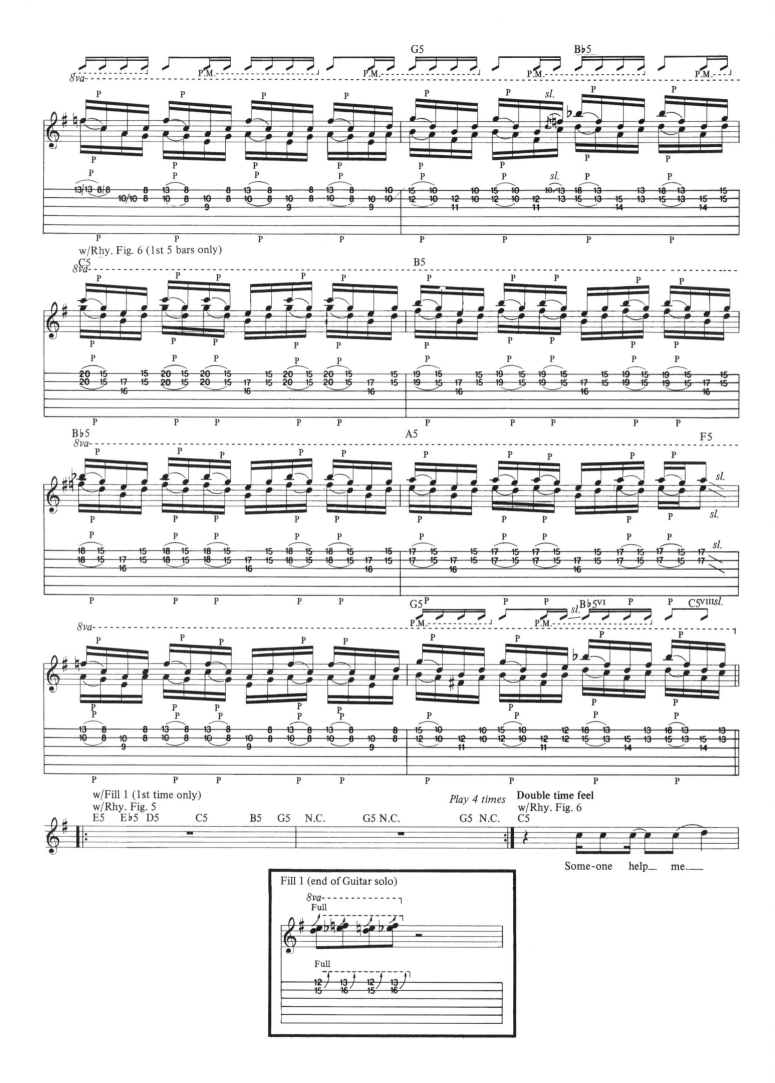

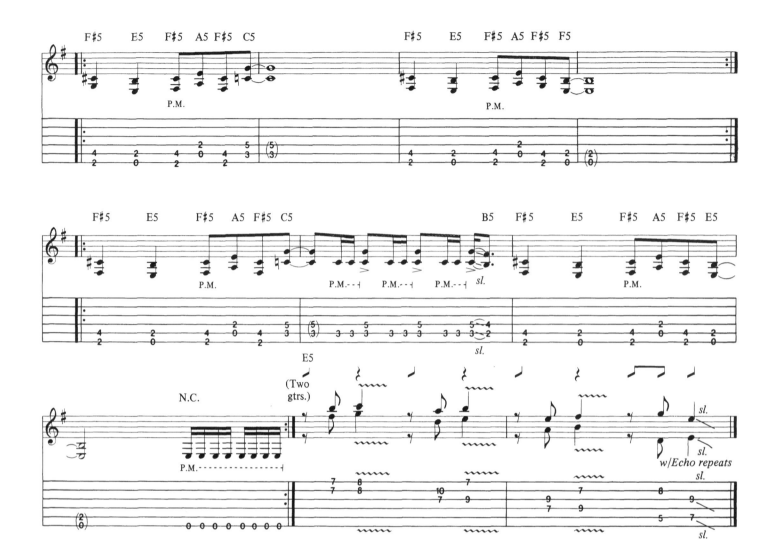

*Additional Lyrics*

2. Wait for the sign
   To flick the switch of death.
   It's the beginning of the end.
   Sweat, chilling cold,
   As I watch death unfold.
   Consciousness my only friend.
   My fingers grip with fear.
   What am I doing here? *(To Chorus)*

3. Time moving slow.
   The minutes seem like hours.
   The final curtain call I see.
   How true is this?
   Just get it over with.
   If this is true, just let it be.
   Wakened by horrid scream.
   Freed from this frightening dream. *(To Chorus)*

# FOR WHOM THE BELL TOLLS

Words and Music by
James Hetfield, Lars Ulrich
and Cliff Burton

1. Make his fight on the hill in the ear-ly day. Con-stant chill deep in-
2. Take a look to the sky just be-fore you die. It's the last time he

side. Shout-ing gun, on they run through the end-less grey.
will. Black-ened roar, mas-sive roar fills the crum-bling sky.

On they fight, for they're right.__ Yes, but who's to say? For a hill men would
Shat-tered goal fills his soul__ with a ruth-less cry. Stran-ger now are his

kill. Why? They do not know. Suf-ferred wounds test their pride.
eyes to this mys-ter-y. Hears the si-lence so loud.

Men of five, still a-live__ through the rag-ing glow. Gone in-sane from the pain__
Crack of dawn, all is gone ex-cept the will to be. Now they see what will be,__

__ that they sure-ly know.} For whom the bell__ tolls.__
__ blind-ed eyes to see.__}

*To Coda*

Time march-es on for whom the bell__ tolls._____

28

# FADE TO BLACK

Words and Music by
James Hetfield, Lars Ulrich,
Cliff Burton and Kirk Hammett

*2nd time substitute Fill 2

Fill 1- - - - - - - - - - - - - - - - - - - - - - - - - - (end Rhy. Fig. 2)

*Use Fill 2 in place of this bar when Rhy.
Fig. 2 is played behind the verse sections.

1st, 2nd Verses
w/Rhy. Fig. 2

1. Life it seems will fade__ a - way, drift - ing fur - ther ev - 'ry day.
2. Things not what they used__ to_ be, miss - ing one in - side__ of me.

Get - ting lost with- in__ my - self,__ noth-ing mat - ters, no__ one_else.
Death - ly lost, this can't_ be real,__ can - not stand this hell__ I __feel.

w/Rhy. Fig. 2 (1st 7 bars only)

I have lost the will__ to_ live, sim - ply noth - ing more__ to give.
Emp - ti - ness is fill - ing__ me__ to the point of ag - o - ny.

There is noth - ing more__ for me.__ Need the end to set
Grow - ing dark - ness tak - ing dawn,__ I was me but now__

Fill 2

Bridge

1. No one but me can save my-self but it's too late._____
2. Yes - ter - day seems as though it nev - er ex - ist - ed._____

Now I can't think, think why I should e - ven___ try._____
Death greets me warm, now I will just say good - bye._____

Rhy. Fill 1 (Gtr. II)

# TRAPPED UNDER ICE

Words and Music by
James Hetfield, Lars Ulrich
and Kirk Hammett

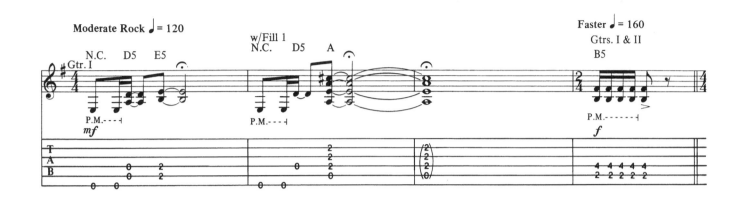

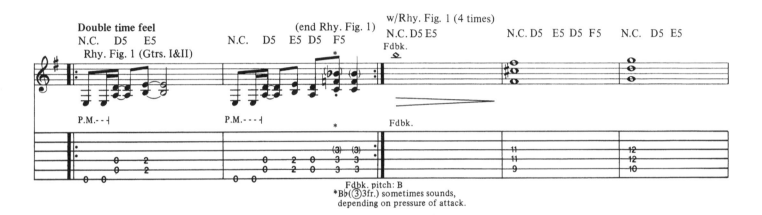

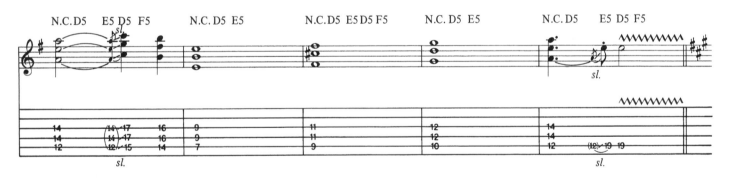

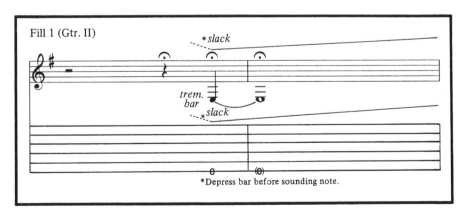

1. I don't know how to live through this hell. Woken up, I'm still locked in this shell.
2.3. *See additional lyrics*

Froz-en soul, froz-en down to the core. Break the ice, I can't take any-more.

*Lightly tap harm. w/L.H. finger.

*Additional Lyrics*

2. Crystalized as I lay here and rest.
   Eyes of glass stare directly at death.
   From deep sleep I have broken away.
   No one knows, no one hears what I say. *(To Chorus)*

3. No release from my cryonic state.
   What is this? I've been stricken by fate.
   Wrapped up tight, cannot move, can't break free.
   Hand of doom has a tight grip on me. *(To Chorus)*

# ESCAPE

Words and Music by
James Hetfield, Lars Ulrich
and Kirk Hammett

true - false world.___  Un - dam-aged des - tin - y.___
so - called stan - dard.  Who says that I ain't right?___

Can't get caught in the end - less cir - cle.  Ring of stu - pid - i - ty.
Break a - way from your com - mon fash - ion.  See through your blur - ry sight.

Chorus

Out___ for my own; out___ to be free. ___

Riff A                    sl.                    (end Riff A)

Rhy. Fig. 2                                    (end Rhy. Fig. 2)

w/Rhy. Fig. 2 & Riff A (both 2 times)

One___ with my mind, they___ just can't see. ___

No___ need to hear things___ that they say. ___

w/Rhy. Fig. 2 & Riff A (both 1st 3 bars only)

Life's___ for my own to live___ my own way. ___

Fill 1

46

Half time feel
Bridge

See them try to bring the ham - mer down.

(end half time feel)

No damn chains can hold me to the ground.

Gtr. solo
w/Rhy. Fig. 3 (4 times)

Rhy. Fig. 3

# CREEPING DEATH

Words and Music by
James Hetfield, Lars Ulrich,
Cliff Burton and Kirk Hammett

*Throughout Rhy. Fig.7, play only lowest note of chord when P.M. is indicated.

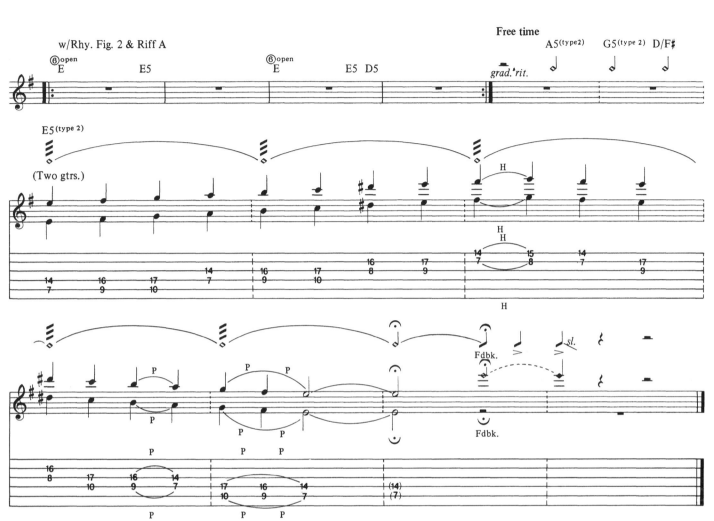

*Additional Lyrics*

2. Now, let my people go, land of Goshen.
Go, I will be with thee, bush of fire.
Blood running red and strong down the Nile.
Plague. Darkness three days long, hail to fire. *(To Chorus)*

3. I rule the midnight air, the destroyer.
Born. I shall soon be there, deadly mass.
I creep the steps and floor, final darkness.
Blood. Lamb's blood, painted door, I shall pass. *(To Chorus)*

# THE CALL OF KTULU

Music by
James Hetfield, Lars Ulrich,
Cliff Burton and Dave Mustaine

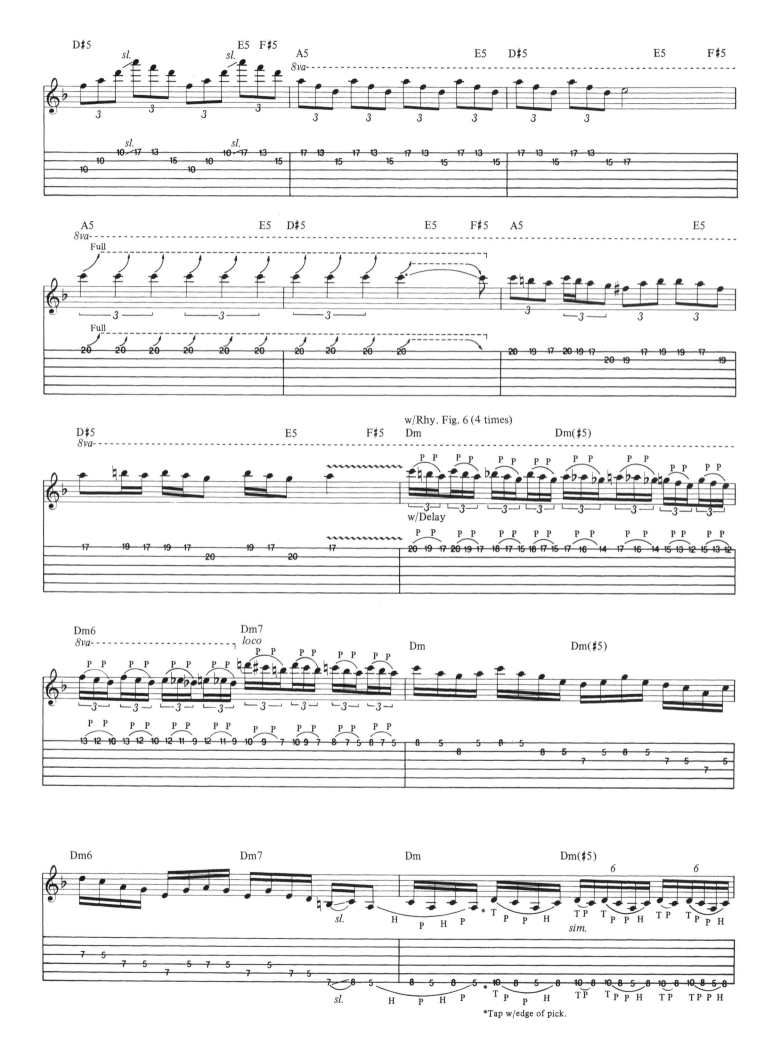

# E-Z PLAY® TODAY SERIES

**OVER 300 VOLUMES AVAILABLE!**

The E-Z Play® Today songbook series is the shortest distance between beginning music and playing fun! Features of this series include:

- full-size books – large 9" x 12" format features easy-to-read, easy-to-play music

- accurate arrangements – simple enough for the beginner, but with authentic-sounding chords and melody lines

- minimum number of page turns

- thousands of songs – an incredible array of favorites, from classical and country to Christmas and contemporary hits

- lyrics – most arrangements include complete song lyrics

- most up-to-date registrations - books in the series contain a general registration guide, as well as individual song rhythm suggestions for today's electronic keyboards and organs

To see full descriptions of all the books in the series, visit:

HAL•LEONARD®

www.halleonard.com